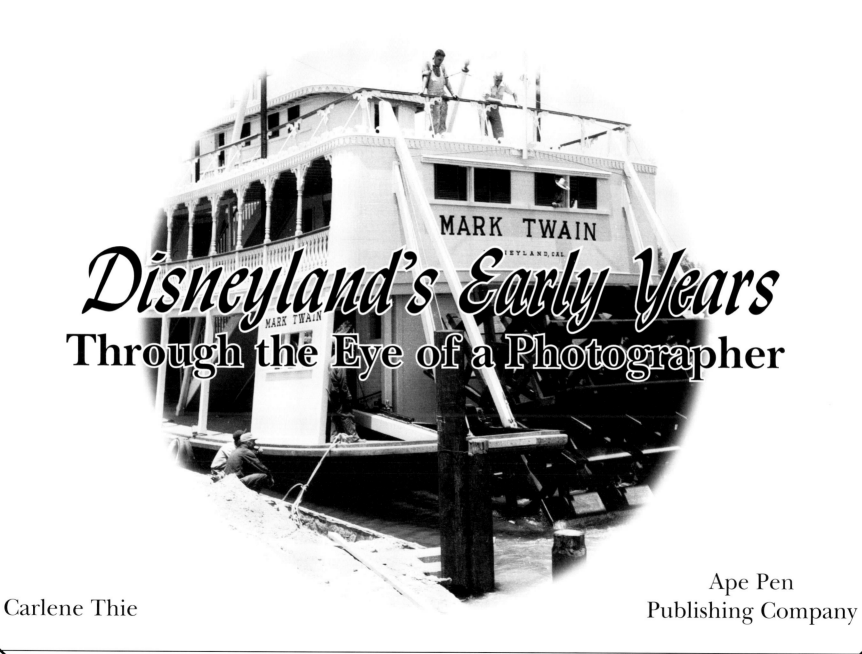

Disneyland's Early Years
Through the Eye of a Photographer

Carlene Thie

Ape Pen
Publishing Company

Photographs by
Mell Kilpatrick

Written and introduced by
Carlene Thie

Disneyland's Early Years
Through the Eye of a Photographer

Third Edition

Ape Pen Publishing Company
Copyright 2003
Volume #2

In memory of Mell Kilpatrick

Mell Kilpatrick 1902-1962

Mell Kilpatrick's passion for photography first started as a hobby. Armed with his "Weegee" style camera, Mell gravitated towards the streets, tracking police calls and showing up at the scene of accidents taking images not meant for the squeamish. He became a familiar figure to the various police departments and insurance companies serving Orange County.

Mell made his way to the Santa Ana Register, contributing his photographic work and working in the darkroom. Eventually he became a member of the photography staff.

Mell started his career as a news photographer at the Santa Ana Register on November 18, 1948 at the age of 40. During his 14 years at the Register, Mell covered Orange County in every possible manner — by air, on foot, by car, and even by boat.

Mell became one of the best known cameramen in Orange County during this time and rose to the position of Chief Photographer. Since Mell never wanted to miss a photo opportunity, he attached to his dash a small camera pointing out of the front windshield of his car. This was fixed up so he could fire the camera while he was driving to make sure he never missed a shot.

With Mell's devotion to his job, and with his ability to capture the images at the right angles, Mell started taking photos of the latest sensation to hit Orange County — the construction of Disneyland. He worked relentlessly to get the perfect shots. Even with Mell being a middle aged man, he would hang out of a light plane standing on its wing 5,000 feet above Disneyland holding a camera which weighed about five pounds. This daring act allowed him to get unique construction views of Disneyland.

Mell went on to take some of the best aerial views of Disneyland's first few years, and thereby captured memories of a time now gone by. On the ground Mell also took hundreds of pre-construction and construction shots of the park.

One year after ground breaking day, on July 17, 1955, Walt Disney's dream finally came true with imagination far exceeding our wildest dreams. Thanks to Mell, these images of the park being built, literally from the ground up, will last forever.

1955 Public Opening Day

Opening:	Monday, July 18, 1955 at 10 am
Location:	1313 Harbor Boulevard, in Anaheim, California
Hours:	10 am to 10 pm seven days a week during the summer. Open 6 days a week in the fall, closed on Mondays.
Founder:	Walt Disney
Area Size:	Total area: 160 acres. Park: 60 acres.
Parking:	Parking lot size: 100 acres. Car capacity: 12,175.
Admission:	$1.00, including tax, for adults and 50 cents, including tax, for children 12 and under.
Food:	20 restaurants in all the four different lands.
Walking:	To visit every land, distance of 1.4 miles.
Personnel:	Over 1,000 employees.
Capacity:	Designed to handle 60,000 visitors daily.
Landscaping:	Plants from all over the world. Approximately 12,000 orange trees removed.

1955

Aerial view of Main Street

Main Street Food and Refreshments 1955

Carnation Company Ice Cream Parlor

Coca-Cola

Maxwell House Division, General Foods

Plaza Pavillion

Swift & Co. Red Wagon Inn

UPT Concessions, Inc. Food Stand in Railroad Station

1959

Main Street from Matterhorn construction

1958

Disneyland's 10-Millionth Visitor Ceremony

1956

Disneyland
Opera House
and
Town Square

1955

Town Square and Mickey Planter

1957

Main Street Trolley stop at Town Square

1956

Disneyland press visitors perusing the Disneyland News

1956

"C'mon Daddy, let's go ride the Rocket to the Moon!"

1955

Walt Disney and
Art Linkletter
discussing the railroad

1955

Firing up the E. P. Ripley from Roundhouse

1958

Busy day on Main Street

1957

Main Street Trolley at Hub stop

Fantasyland Food and Refreshments 1955

Chicken of the Sea, Pirate Ship

UPT Concessions, Inc. Food Stand

Welch Grape Juice Company

1955

Aerial view of Fantasyland

1956

Sleeping Beauty Castle from Snow Mountain

1957

Sleeping Beauty Castle
from
Plaza Gardens

1957

Sleeping Beauty Castle
night view

1957

Sleeping Beauty Castle
from
Fantasyland

1955

Casey Junior
Railroad Station

1955

Casey Junior "Wild Animals" Cage Car

1961

Skull Rock in Fantasyland

1955

The backside of Fantasyland

1959

Fantasyland from Matterhorn construction

1959

Story Book Land from Matterhorn construction

Tomorrowland Food and Refreshments 1955

UPT Concessions, Inc. - Space Bar

1955

Tomorrowland aerial view

1959

Tomorrowland from the air, 101 Freeway in foreground

1959

Aerial view of Matterhorn

1955

Court of Honor Flags in Tomorrowland

1955

Interior of Kelvinator Circarama Theater

1960

Bell Telephone Theater, with Time Clock of the World

1960

"America the Beautiful" - Bell Telephone Theater

1959

Submarine Voyage being checked out

1959

Submarine Voyage inspection — Skipjack and Ethan Allen

Frontierland Food and Refreshments 1955

Fritos — Frito House

Pepsi Cola — Golden Horseshoe

Quaker Oats — Aunt Jemima's Kitchen

Swift's — Chicken Plantation

UPT Concessions, Inc. — Food stands

UPT Concessions, Inc. — Malt shop

1956

Aerial View of Frontierland

1955

Mark Twain docked in Fowler's Harbor

1955

Testing Mark Twain Steamboat paddlewheel

1955

Mark Twain Steamboat at Magnolia Park

1955

Mark Twain at dock with Straw Hatters playing at the bandstand

1956

Rivers of America from Indian Village

1956

Tom Sawyer's Island

1955

Cast of Golden Horseshoe Review

1955

Hamming it up on stage at the Golden Horseshoe Review

1958

Pack Mules and Disneyland Stagecoach Lines at Rainbow Ridge

1958

Pack Mules heading onto Rainbow Ridge

1956

Casa de Fritos

1956

Casa de Fritos with Frito Kid

1958

Aerial view of Frontierland from Holidayland

1958

Rivers of America from Holidayland

1955

Fess Parker
at
Davy Crockett
Arcade

1955

Rehearsal for opening day in Frontierland

1958

Jimmy Durante entertaining on the radio live from Frontierland

1956

Drummers for Indian Village in Frontierland

1956

Indian Village
in
Frontierland

1956

Tribal Dancers at Indian Village

Adventureland Food and Refreshments 1955

Pavillion

Tropical "Saloon"

1956

Aerial View of Adventureland

1955

Jungle Cruise Ride loading dock

1955

Native hut on Jungle Cruise Ride

1956

Schweitzer Falls
on
Jungle Cruise

1956

Approaching Schweitzer Falls

1955

Crocodiles ready to go

1955

Jungle Cruise rhino and alligator

1955

Rhino on Jungle Cruise

1955

Charging rhino on Jungle Cruise

1955

Jungle Cruise hippo surfaces

1955

Elephant on Jungle Cruise

1955

Jungle Cruise Ride

1955

Jungle Cruise hippos ready for water

As people touched my life with their love of Disneyland, I realized I could contribute to their memories by creating these photo books which capture Disneyland's early history for everyone to enjoy. More importantly, by sharing these images, I am able to honor my grandfather, and his legacy as a photojournalist. Through these projects, I have met many wonderful people, and learned a great deal about Walt Disney and his dreams — for this I am very grateful.

Carlene Thie

Author and Publisher
Carlene Thie
with "Ape" April (Actress)

Vol. # 1

**A photographer's life with
Disneyland Under Construction**

Vol. # 2

**Disneyland's Early Years
Through the Eye of a Photographer**

Vol. # 3

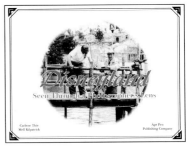

**Disneyland
Seen Through a Photographer's Lens**

I want to thank God and all those who have helped me in the process of creating these volumes, especially my family.

Copyright 2003 - Ape Pen Publishing

P.O. Box 691, Riverside, California 92502
ApePenPublishing.com

*Printed in U.S.A.
by Jostens, Inc.
Marceline, Missouri*